Python

AZ Elite Publishing

Published by
AZ Elite Publishing
www.AZElitePublishing.GR8.com

ISBN-13: 978-1505549683
ISBN-10: 150554968X

Manufactured in Canada
Published simultaneously in Canada

Notice of Liability:

TABLE OF CONTENTS

Chapter 1: Jumping into Python

So, your interested in learning Python? Python is a cutting edge programming language that is geared toward simplicity. Python was created to be written productively with maximum readability, without having to sacrifice quality. If you're reading this book, you've probably already researched Python and have a good idea of what the language could potentially offer. Well, the hype is true. The language has received increased attention in recent years for a good reason – it's easy to learn, it's extremely readable, and the software quality it creates is unmatched.

"Python is fast enough for our site and allows us to produce maintainable features in record times, with a minimum of developers," said Cuong Do, software architect for YouTube.com.

Even if you have never written a single line of code in your life, Python is an excellent place to start learning. One great thing about programming is that all languages are very similar to one another. Sure, they all have different syntax and different features, but generally programming code transplanted from one language to another will look very similar. If you learn the introductory concepts in one language, you can easily apply it to other languages as well. Likewise, if you are coming to Python with a background in a different language, you should find the transition relatively easy.

Your typical Python program will contain one-third the code of your typical C++ or Java program, which is one of the reasons why it has become so popular in recent years. There is simply less code (without sacrificing the readability of the language), and this leads to less debugging and fewer errors to sort out. Python can be used to program virtually anything.

The History of Python

Python was first created in the late 1980s by Guido van Rossum at CWI, located in the Netherlands. In the beginning, the development of the language started as a hobby for Rossum, originally meant to kill some time during a winter vacation. The 2nd version of the language, Python 2.0 was released in 2000, kick starting its popularity. The release of the second version came with increased transparency and community participation in the development process. Python 3 made its debut in 2008, and originally was not backwards-compatible, which hindered its growth. Since then, the language has been back ported to work with previous versions of the language. In this book we will be covering Python 2 exclusively, as Python 3 has not been adopted by most large organizations at this time.

Benefits of Python

Python was originally developed to be a simpler, more readable programming language that didn't sacrifice functionality. Today Python is more popular than ever, and has become known for;

- **Software Quality.** Python code is stripped down. It's simple, but its efficient. For this reason, programs written in Python are typically a higher level of quality.
- **Portability.** Python as a language hasn't changed all of that much over the years and for that reason, it is extremely portable. You could copy code from a program written 10 years ago, and paste it into a program today without an issue.
- **Library Support.** Libraries are community-created, pre-built functions. There is nearly an unlimited number of Python libraries available today, each bringing its own benefits to the table.
- **It's fun.** Python strips the code down and uses indentations instead of brackets to determine what is run and when. This, combined with its built-in toolset make it a joy to code, which has brought many new users on board.

Chapter 2: Getting Started

Its time to get to know Python! There will be a few resources that you need to know about before we dive head-first into the code. We'll start by installing the best IDE for Python use, PyCharm.

"Python has been an important part of Google since the beginning, and remains so as the system grows and evolves. Today dozens of Google engineers use Python, and we're looking for more people with skills in this language." - Peter Norvig, director of search at Google.

Installing Python and an IDE

Python is relatively easy to install, and doesn't require a whole lot of knowledge. Navigate to the download page located here:

https://www.python.org/download/releases/2.7.8/

This is the most used version of Python. Make sure that you download the correct file, based on your operating system.

Open the installation file and click "Install for all users."

Installing an IDE

For an IDE, we will be using PyCharm. You can access their download page here:

http://www.jetbrains.com/pycharm/download/

PyCharm is one of the most popular IDE's for Python. It's simple, easy to use, and comes with a built in command prompt, which truly simplifies things for beginners. The best feature is that the community edition is available completely for free, offering all of the standard features for Python development. Make sure to select your operating system from the tabs at the top of the page before downloading. Your download will be more than 100 MB, so it could take some time to complete. The installation process is relatively straight forward.

Example Program

You'll be shocked by how little code is actually required when programming in Python. Compared to other languages, you might see half (or less) of the total number of lines of code. But don't mistake that for a lack of depth. Python is robust, with enough features for companies like Google and Facebook to choose Python as a primary language for some of their largest business processes.

Remember that Python in its simplest form is nothing more than a text file with Python statements. If you are coming to Python from C# and other similar languages, executing files is a bit different in Python, and often a less visual process.

Here I will walk you through the creation of a sample

program. It will be your typical "Hello, World" opener that you've likely seen before.

Step 1: Open PyCharm.

Step 2: Go to File > New Project

Step 3: In the "Project name:" section, enter "HelloPythonWorld", then click OK. Make sure you have the correct interpreter selected.

Step 4: In the project window, right click on the folder named "HelloPython World" and select New > Python File. When prompted, name the file "HelloP".

Step 5: Copy and paste the following code into the text editor:

print "Hello, World!"

Step 6: In the "Run" Menu, click "Run".

Step 7: You will be prompted to specify what you would like to run. Select "HelloP".

Step 8: Look at the logs that were generated after running the program. It doesn't look like much. You should be seeing something like this;

While this not seem like anything significant, the logs have signaled that the program ran correctly. This is excellent! However, many users will prefer to see a visual representation of their program. Here's a simple way to do so;

Step 9: Click your start button. Use the search function (or manually navigate) to the "Python (command line)" program.

Step 10: Once the command prompt opens, type the same line of code from step 5 into the command prompt.

This gives you a good overview of how to go about creating a project and watching it run. Unlike other programming languages, Python doesn't need or utilize a graphical user interface when running a program. This can be confusing for those that are coming over from other visual programming languages, but ultimately doesn't effect much.

Chapter 3: Building Our First Programs

Now that we have seen Python in action, it's time to dive in head first. Before coding our own program, there are a few things that need to be understood about the language to make the early learning process go as seamlessly as possible.

> "One of my most productive days was throwing away 1000 lines of code" - Ken Thompson

Indentation

One of the first caveats that experienced programmers run into when making the switch to Python is the fact that the language does not use braces to indicate blocks of code – instead all blocks of code are denoted by indentation. This indentation is a strict function of the language. If you indent the wrong number of spaces – the program won't run correctly.

In Python, the number of spaces for indentations is variable. However, all of the statements within a single block of code have to be intended the same amount. To drive this point home, the following code would run fine;

```
if True:
        print "True"
else:
  print "False"
```

Notice that both "print" statements are indented different amounts. This is fine, because they are two separate blocks of code. Here's an example of incorrectly indented code;

```
if True:
        print "Answer"
        print "True"
else:
        print "Answer"
    print "False"
```

This block of code wouldn't run correctly. Both "print" commands inside the "else" statement belong to one block of code, but are not indented the same amount. This causes the interpreter to regard "print "False"" as if it were it's own statement, outside of the "else" statement's influence.

Variables

All programming languages available today use data types as a way to store information, categorized by similarities. Like many other languages, Python uses the standard data types.

These include;

Numbers

Number data types are used to store numeric values. Unlike other languages that include several different data types for storing numbers based on storage needs, Python creates a new object with a new memory allocation for larger numbers. Although for our purposes you won't have to worry about individual number data types, the different numerical types include;

- int (signed integers)
- long (long integers)
- float (floating point values)
- complex (complex numbers)

Numbers do not require that you name the data type. Here is an example of assigning a number to a variable;

```
var1 = 3
var2 = 5
```

Now "var 1"holds the value 3, and "var 2"holds the value 5.

Strings

Phrases or words are stored as strings. Strings are always within quotations. Anything inside of quotation marks is considered to be a string, whether or not it is assigned to a variable. Some examples of the different ways in which strings are used include;

```
str = 'Hello World!'
```

```
print str          # Prints complete string

print str[0]        # Prints first character of the string

print str[2:5]      # Prints characters starting from 3rd to
5th

print str[2:]       # Prints string starting from 3rd
character

print str * 3       # Prints string three times

print str + "YOYO"  # Prints concatenated string
```

These commands would produce an output that looks like:

```
Hello World!
H
llo
llo World!
Hello World!Hello World!Hello World!
Hello World!YOYO
```

- Lists: Python lists provide very versatile ways to store lists of items. A list contains items that are separated by commas and enclosed within brackets. There are multiple ways to access information that is stored within lists. Here are some examples of the more popular ways to use strings:

```
list = [ 'abcd', 786 , 2.23, 'john', 70.2 ]
tinylist = [123, 'john']
print list       # Prints complete list
print list[0]    # Prints first element of the list
print list[1:3]  # Prints elements starting from 2nd till
3rd
print list[2:]   # Prints elements starting from 3rd
element
print tinylist * 2  # Prints list two times
print list + tinylist # Prints concatenated lists
```

Which would produce the following results;

```
['abcd', 786, 2.23, 'john', 70.200000000000003]
abcd
[786, 2.23]
[2.23, 'john', 70.200000000000003]
[123, 'john', 123, 'john']
['abcd', 786, 2.23, 'john', 70.200000000000003, 123,
'john']
```

- Tuples: In many ways, Tuples are similar to lists. They contain a number of values that are separated by commas. Unlike lists, Tuples have their data enclosed within parenthesis instead of brackets. Tuples are not able to have their values updated.
- Dictionary: A Python dictionary is a table. They are very similar to arrays and can be

used to store large amounts of data. There is no order within dictionaries.

Operators

Operators are used to change or check the value of a provided piece of data. There are many different types of operators including arithmetic operators (+, -, /, %. *), comparison operators, assignment operators, logical operators, bitwise operators, membership operators and identity operators. For our purposes today, we will simply focus on arithmetic operators and comparison operators.

The Different types of arithmetic operators include;

- $\pm$ - Addition. Adds two values on either side of the operator together.
    - $\underline{-}$ - Subtraction. Subtracts right side from left side.
- - Multiplication. Multiplies values on both sides of the operator together.
- $\underline{/}$ - Division. Divides left hand side from right hand side.
- $\underline{\%}$ - Modulus. Divides left hand side from right hand side and returns the remainder

The Different types of comparison operators include;
- == - Checks to see if two values on either side are equal or not. If they are then the condition returns true.
- != - Checks to see if two values on either side are equal or not. If they are not, the condition returns true.
    - ➤ - Greater than.
- < - Less than.
- >= - Greater than or equal to.
- <= - Less than or equal to.

PROJECT: Variables

Try to complete this project on your own without looking at the answer.

Create 2 numbers and 2 strings. Add the numbers together and then print the total. Then, display the strings four times a piece.

Answer

```
var1 = 3
var2 = 5
str1 = "Testing"
str2 = "Testing2"
var3 = var1 + var2
print(var3)
print str1 *4
print str2 * 4
```

Now you should have an understanding of the basic set of operators that are available to you. Think about the different ways in which these could be used, and how you might manipulate or check data using them. Now we will put these to use using decision making statements;

Conditional Operators (If/Else Statements)

Python also makes use of decision making statements. These structures allow the programmer to specify one or more conditions that will be tested by the program. The program will determine if the statement is true, and execute the code given. If the statement is false, the programmer may also provide additional statements and code to run. Python uses a number of different types of decision making statements;

If Statement

If statements allow the program to check to see whether a statement is true, and then execute code that corresponds with a true statement. Here is an example of an if statement;

```
var = 55
if ( var  == 55 ) : print "Value of expression is 55"
print "Good bye!"
```

This If Statement checks to see if the variable "var" is equal to 55. If the value of "var" is 55, then it will print the expression "Value of expression is 55". Should the variable not be equal to 55, the program would only print "Good Bye!"

If/Else Statement.

An If statement can also include another path for the program to take. In the previous example, had the var stored a value of 87, the program would have not run any code, except for saying "Good bye!" The else statement contains code that runs should the boolean expression returned by the If statement be false. Here is an example of an if/else statement;

```
temperature = float(input('What is the temperature? '))
if temperature > 65:
    print('Wear shorts.')
```

```
else:
    print('Wear jeans.')
    print('Enjoy the sun.')
```

This program begins by prompting the user to tell them what the temperature is. The user enters the temperature, which is stored in a float variable named "temperature." This variable is then checked by the program. The If Statement states that if the temperature provided by the user is higher than 65, print the line "Wear shorts." Keep in mind that there can be multiple if statements in the same block of code. When that happens, you use the term "elif" which stands for "elseif." In example:

```
temperature = float(input('What is the temperature? '))
if temperature < 50:
        print('Bundle Up')
elif temperature > 75:
        print('Go Swimming.')
else:
    print('Either Or')
```

This program instructs the computer to print "Bundle up" when the temperature is below 50, "Go Swimming" when the temperature is above 75, and "Either Or" when the temperature is between 50 and 75.

This is where the Else Statement comes in. The Else Statement only comes into play if the temperature is not higher than 65, so the Boolean expression returned by the If Statement is False. If the user entered a temperature of 64, then the program would print "Wear jeans." Regardless of what the user enters, the program prints "Enjoy the sun."

Nested Statements

It is also important to note that If/Else Statements can be nested inside of one another. Consider the last example. What if we wanted the program to instruct the user to go shirtless if the temperature was over 80 degrees? We could nest a new if statement within the previous statement. It would look like this;

```
temperature = float(input('What is the temperature? '))
humidity = float(input('What is the humidity? '))
if temperature > 65:
    print('Wear shorts.')
    if humidity >= 80:
        print('Go Shirtless.')
else:
    print('Wear jeans.')
print('Enjoy the sun.')
```

This program adds a new conditional statement into the mix. Now, it asks the user two questions. First, they provide the temperature. Then, they provide the humidity. If the temperature is both over 65 degrees and over 80 humidity, the program tells them to wear shorts, and go shirtless. Should the user enter a temperature of 70 and a humidity of 60, the program would just tell the user to wear shorts.

PROJECT: Decision Making

Now that you are familiar with decision making statements, it's time for you to try it on your own. Try to complete the project on your own without looking at the answer. Create a program that asks the user for the time (1-24). Depending on what time it is, print a different phrase. If the time is before 10, print "Good Morning." If the time is before 19, print "Good Day." If the time is after 19, print "Good Night."

Answer

```
time = float(input('What time is it? (1-24) '))
if time < 10:
        print "Good morning"
elif time < 19:
        print "Good day"
else
        print "Good night"
```

Loops

Loops are present in every programming language. Loops exist to allow a program to execute a certain block of code a specified number of times. Within a loop, the code is executed one run after another. The program stays within a loop until it has run a specified amount of times. There can be multiple statements within a loop. The following types of loops are present in the Python Programming Language;

While Loops

The while loop allows the program to repeat a statement or several statements while a condition is true. The condition is tested by the program before executing the statement. Here is an example of a While Loop;

```
counter = 0

while (counter < 8):

    print 'The counter is:', count

    counter = counter + 1
```

This program sets counter to 0. Then, while counter is equal to less than 8, it prints the value of the counter variable and adds one to it each time the code is run. The result in your logs should look like this;

```
The counter is: 0
The counter is: 1
The counter is: 2
The counter is: 3
The counter is: 4
The counter is: 5
The counter is: 6
The counter is: 7
```

You can also use Else Statements inside of loops. In loops, else statements work exactly the same way as they do in if statements. If the condition is returned as False, the program is provided another path to take. Here is an an example of a While Loop with an Else Statement;

```
counter = 0
while counter < 8:
    print counter, " is  less than 8"
    count = counter + 1
else:
    print counter, " is not less than 8"
```

This program sets counter to 0. While counter is less than 8, the While loop is looped by the program. It prints the value of the counter, and adds one to it each time. Once the loop has run and counter is equal to 8, then the else statement will run. When run, the logs look something like this;

```
0 is less than 8
1 is less than 8
2 is less than 8
3 is less than 8
4 is less than 8
5 is less than 8
6 is less than 8
7 is less than 8
8 is not less than 8
```

For Loops

For loops are very similar to While Loops. They allow you to repeat a piece of code a number of times. Here is an example of a For Loop;

```
for count in [1, 2, 3]:
    print(count)    print('Python' * count)
print('Done counting.')
for color in ['red', 'blue', 'green']:
    print(color)
```

This program uses the count function, and lists three numbers. The first For Loop will cycle through 3 times, one for each number listed. Each time it will print the count, and print the word Python that many times. When finished, the program prints "Done Counting." The log output for this program looks like this;

```
1
Python
2
PythonPython
3
PythonPythonPython
Done counting.
red
blue
green
```

PROJECT: Loops

Now you are familiar with Loops, so let's test your skills with a project. Try not to look at the answer until you have finished your own program. In this project we will count by two's, up to 100. Set a number variable named "num1" to 2. Use a While Loop to add 2 to num1 every time it loops and display the number. When 100 is reached, the program should say "100! I've just learned the basics of Python!"

Answer:

```
num1 = 2
while num1 < 100:
    print num1
    num1 = num1 + 2
else:
    print num1, "! I've just learned the basics of Python!"
```

Chapter 4: Lists and Tuples

Now that we have built our first program, let's look at some of the more advanced concepts of the language. Python is an in-depth language that provides plenty of functionality, but advanced concepts can get a little overwhelming. Lists are a simple step forward that teaches you some advanced concepts without presenting too much information in one fell swoop.

> "A programming language is low level when its programs require attention to the irrelevant."
> - Alan J. Perlis.

What Are Lists?

Lists allow you to deal with multiple different data items and process them in a sequence. As we went over earlier, there are multiple different data types that contain more than one item. These include;

- Strings (pieces of text)

- Tuples (lists and ordered groups of several individual items of data)
- Dictionaries (groups of key-value pairs)

These are the most commonly used data types that are able to store multiple different data items. This data can then be accessed using an index.

Accessing Items

Individual items that are contained within a sequence can be obtained using an index. Basically, an index is a number that corresponds with where the data is stored within the sequence. Accessing items that are contained within a tuple is done in the same way that you would access items of any other data type as well. Here is an example of accessing items in a list of tuple;

```
fruits = ['apples', 'bananas', 'oranges', 'grapes', 'mangos']
fruits[2]
'oranges'
```

Each item contained within the list is represented by a number. The first item in all lists is referred to as "0". In this example, Apples are 0, bananas are 1, oranges are 2, grapes are 3, and mangoes are 4. You can call on the program to display any of the different fruits, based on where they are contained within the list. There are many ways in which you can access and utilize this data as well, slicing, and pulling individual pieces of data out of each of the data containers within the list. Here is an example of pulling multiple different pieces of data out of a list;

```
fruits = ['apples', 'bananas', 'oranges', 'grapes', 'mangos']
fruits[2:4]
['oranges', 'mangos']
```

In this example you call on both 2 and 4, displaying both
oranges and mangoes. Accessing items in lists is consistent
and quite simple. You can use the same commands across
multiple data types, which makes the entire process much
easier to handle.

Boolean Statements and Lists

You can also pull boolean statements from lists as well. This
is great for situations where you want to check the contents
of a list of tuple. Sticking with the fruits example, you can ask
the program to check your given list and return whether or
not it contains the data that you are looking for.

Does the List contain raspberry?

'raspberry' in fruits

False

You can also ask it the other way around.

'raspberry' not in fruits

True

**You can also check for specific inclusions in different
data containers.**

'ana' in 'banana'

True

Creating Tuples

Tuples as a data type are often used in conjunction with, or to replace lists. Tuples are immutable ordered groups of items or elements. Think of them like containers. Every tuple is made up of many individuals containers that contain data. You specify which container you wou8ld like to access when accessing the data, and then may use that data in a variety of different ways. They are comma-separated lists of values that are enclosed within parenthesis.

Creating a tuple is simple. Here is a command that allows you to create a tuple;

```
blank_tuple = ()
```

You have now created a tuple named "blank_tuple"that contains no data as of yet. Remember that all items contained within a tuple must be followed by a comma, even if they are the only item within the tuple. So a tuple that contains a single item would have (item1,) within the parenthesis. Tuples are accessed in the same way that lists are accessed.

Creating Lists

Lists are the most common method for storing multiple values in Python. They are an ordered, comma-separated list that are enclosed within brackets. Lists are different because they can store many different items –they all do not have to be the same data type. Here are some examples provided in an earlier chapter about using lists;

```
print str        # Prints complete string
```

```
print str[0]      # Prints first character of the string
print str[2:5]    # Prints characters starting from 3rd to 5th
print str[2:]     # Prints string starting from 3rd character
print str * 3     # Prints string three times
print str + "YOYO" # Prints concatenated string
```

Here are some methods that can be used to append, change, and edit lists that have already been created. These are extremely useful for manipulating data that is already contained within the list, once it has been declared.

list.append(X) −Add an item to the end of your list.

List.extend(L) −This extends the list by appending all of the items that are already contained within the list.

List.insert(i, x) −The insert command allows you to insert an item at a given position. You can choose to insert a new piece of data into the middle of the list, pushing everything behind it farther down.

List.remove(X) −Remove an item from your list, in the position represented by x.

list.pop([i]) −Remove an item from the list at the specified postion and return it. If you do not specify a position, the last item in the list will be removed and returned.

List.index(x) −The index command returns the item at the index location that you have called on.

List.reverse() - Reverses all elements within the list.

All off these commands are great ways to append, change,

and edit a list that you have already created. You will find that frequently you may want to add item sto a list, or edit data already placed within the list based on the actions of your user.

PROJECT: Lists and Tuples

Now you are familiar with lists and tuples, so let's test your skills with a project. Try not to look at the answer until you have finished your own program. In this project we will be making a camping checklist. Create a list named "camping" and include tent, swimwear, cooking supplies, and a first aid kit. Use the append command to add life-jackets. Then, insert hiking boots into position 3 on your list, and display the list.

Answer:

```
camping = ['tent', 'swimwear', 'cooking supplies', 'first aid kit']
camping.append('lifejackets')
camping.insert(3, 'hiking boots')
print camping
```

Chapter 5: Functions

Functions are the bread and butter of any large-scale program. All fo the examples that we have worked on through this point have been top-down. This means that the programs begins at the top of the page and executes through the bottom of the page. Functions allow you to create and call on code located elsewhere, throughout the whole of your program. This makes it easy to re-use code several times throughout a program.

> "Talk is cheap. Show me the code."
> - Linus Torvalds

What Are Functions?

Functions are pieces of code that can be called to within your program. They are used to break up code and call on certain code as needed. For instance, in most top-down programs, you may need to use the same piece of code several times. This means that when you change the functionality of the program, you ma have to edit the same block of code several times throughout the program. But, by creating a function – you can then call on that code several times throughout the program. Later, when you decide to change the functionality of that program, you only have to edit the code once to make changes to multiple code blocks within the program. A function is a block of organized, re-usable code that can be used throughout a program.

All programming languages contain functions in one form or another. Functions are defined in our code using a def statement. This statement is followed by the name of the function, with some parameters outlined in parenthesis.

Defining Functions

Functions must be defined to create and use certain functionality. There are many functions that come built in with the language (such as the print function, for instance), but you can also define your own. When defining functions there are multiple things that need to be noted;

- Function blocks always begin with "def"to define the function.
- All input parameters and arguments must be placed within the parenthesis when you define a function.
- The code block always comes after a colon (:).
- Using the statement "return"will cause you to exit the function.

Here is an example of defining a function;

```
function_name(parameters)
```

Defining a function is simple.

Parameters and Returning Functions

When your computer runs a function, it does not see the function name, but rather what the function executed. This means that functions just return the values that they are supposed to, and the names of items defined within the parameters can not be called from elsewhere in the program until they were turned. To make this a bit easier to understand, let's pretend that the function that we have created uses this code;

```
A = multiply(5)
```

Now, keep in mind that the multiply function is not a pre-defined function, so this code will not work unless you create it yourself. The program would likely return something like this;

```
a = 25
```

This is all that the program would see when you call on the function, and is the only data point that you have available to use throughout the rest of your programs. It ran the function and returned a piece of data based on the parameters that it was given within the code.

Example Function

Now lets check out functions in action so you can visually see how they work within a program. Here is an example function that you can enter into your IDE;

```
def hello():
        print "hello"
```

```
return 1234
```

To call this function, you use this code:

```
print hello()
```

When you call the "hello()"function, the program will output the following values;

```
hello

1234
```

So what exactly is going on here? A number of things are happening. We are creating a function, calling that function, and observing the output. Keep in mind that in this example, while the program prints both "hello"and "1234,"it actually does not know that "hello"was printed within the function. The program will only be aware of the value that is returned, which in this case is 1234.

Passing Parameters in Functions

Parameters can also be passed to functions as well, and often are. In our example earlier in the chapter, you were given the following line as the basic was to define functions;

```
function_name(parameters)
```

We will now go over the usage of parameters when defining functions. The parameters that you place in the parenthesis will be usable by the function itself. Perhaps you have created data that will need to be used within the function? You can pass all sorts of data types to the functions. Here is an example program that allows you to see how defining a function and passing parameters might work in your program.

```
w = 4
h = 5
Def area(w,h):
        return w * h
print area()
```

This program applies width and height values to the parameters w and h. These parameters are then used in the creation of the function "area." This function multiples width by height, returning the value. The program calls on this function, and then prints the value returned. The output should be "20".

Variables in Functions

Variables are often used in functions. The same variables may be used several times throughout a Python program. The language has a unique way of dealing with this situations. So far we have only be using global variables. Global variables are accessible throughout the entirety of the program. But, functions have their own special types of variables. These are called local variables.

What this means is that you could have two variables with the same name, for the sake of clarity, lets pretend that we have both a global variable named "a"and a local variable named "a"located inside of a function.

Here is an example that demonstrates how this might work inside of a program;

```
a = 2
def print_a():
a = 5
print"int  print_func a = ", a
print_a()
print"a = ", a,"is a global variable assigned prior to the
function print_a"
```

This then outputs:

```
Int print_a a = 5
a = 2 is a global variable assigned prior to the function
print_a
```

a = 2 was defined outside of the function, and therefore is a global variable. The local variable that is located inside of the function has the same name, but has been assigned a different value. The local variable inside of the function can only be called within that function, and never outside of it. The global variable can be called anywhere within the program at any time.

Variable assignments inside of a function will never overwrite the global variables that have already been declared. For all intents and purposes –local variables exist only inside of a function.

PROJECT: Functions

Now you are familiar with functions, so let's test your skills with a project. Try not to look at the answer until you have finished your own program. In this project we will be create a meal planning program. Prompt the user to enter whether they want a low calorie, or high calorie meal. Create functions for both types of meals. If they choose a low calorie meal, print "chef salad with low-fat dressing" and return the value 4.99 (the price). If they choose the high calorie meal, print "cheeseburger with french fries" and return the value 6.99.

Answer:

```
lowprice = 4.99
highprice = 6.99
def low(lowprice,):
    print "Chef salad with low-fat dressing"
    return lowprice
def high(high,):
    print "Cheeseburger with French Fries"
    return highprice
meal = float(input('Enter 1 for a low calorie meal or 2 for a high calorie meal'))
if meal == 1:
    print low(lowprice)
else:
    print high(high)
```

Chapter 6: Classes

Now that you have a basic understanding of functions, it's time to start putting it all together with classes. Classes expand upon the functionality provided by functions. They allow for greater flexibility, and can help to reduce lines of code in your program.

> "In theory, theory and practice are the same. In practice, they're not."
> - Yoggi Berra

What Are Classes?

Classes are in a way very similar to functions. Unfortunately, there are some holes in the functionality of functions. They can not store or save any information –like variables. Every time that a function is run, it starts anew –completely fresh. Classes are most often used when you need your function to actually effect the variables and parameters that you are sending it –rather than just spitting out a return value.

If you were creating a program that calculated and stored the value of all of your assets, you will need to change variables over time. Some of your assets will depreciate, requiring that the variables stored within functions are altered. What if you purchased additional assets that needed to be added to a list? Maybe you invested in new features (like an addition to a home) that requires that the assets value change over time. It's for situations like the ones we just mentioned that object-oriented-programming was created.

Classes are typically used after writing several functions that manipulate similar sets of data, or global variables. When several functions are altering the same data, it is best that they be grouped together as multiple different aspects of a single objec (a class, in this case).

A class is a blueprint. On it's own, it is not much of anything. Classes contain a number of statements that provide instructions. Variables can be altered within classes.

Defining and Creating Classes

Defining and creating classes is actually very similar to defining and creating functions. Here is the basic layout for creating a class;

```
# Defining a class
class class_name:
[statement 1]
[statement 2]
[statement 3]
[etc]
```

Now let's get a little bit more in depth. Here is a class that would be used in a basic banking program. This class instructs the program how to go about displaying the balance, depositing, withdrawing, and overdrawing accounts. It then prints the overall balance of the bank account after withdrawing 5 from it.

```
Class BankAccount(object):
    def __init__(self, initial_balance=0):
        self.balance = initial_balance
    def deposit(self, amount):
        self.balance += amount
    def withdraw(self, amount):
        self.balance -= amount
    def overdrawn(self):
        return self.balance < 0
my_account = BankAccount(15)
my_account.withdraw(5)
print my_account.balance
```

Notice how the class contains several different functions within it? The deposit, withdraw, and overdrawn functions all provide different instructions for the program, while altering variables, which would not be possible if this same program was laid out in several different functions. This allows several different functions to alter a variable that is local to the class that you have defined.

Class Terminology

There are a few different terms that you need to understand when using classes, related to object oriented programming.

- **Class** – A user-defined prototype for an object that defines a number of different attributes.
- **Class variable** – A variable that is present within a class, and is shared by all instances of that class. They are defined within the class, but not within the methods or functions that they class contains.
- **Data Member** – A class variable that holds data associated with the class and its objects.
- **Instance Variable** – A variable that is defined inside of a method or function. It only exists within that function or variable.
- **Method** – A special function that is defined within a class.
- **Object** – A unique instance of data that is defined by the class.

Using Classes and Self

After creating classes, then you can use them throughout the entirety of your program. Classes can be called at any time throughout the program. You can also access attributes of the class from outside the instance, which allows you to use, alter, and manipulate variables used by the class from elsewhere within your program.

One of the main differences between methods and function is the parameter self. "Self"refers to the main object that is being altered by an operation. Using the self parameter is a catch-all for whatever is being altered within the class.

PROJECT: Classes

Now you are familiar with classes, so let's test your skills with a project. Try not to look at the answer until you have finished your own program. In this project we will be create a class that stores employ information. This class will contain 3 functions. The first function (__init__) will store the name, salary and total employee count. The second class, displayCount will display the total employee count, and the third class, displayEmployee, will display all of the recorded information on a given employee

Answer:

```
class Employee:
    'Common base class for all employees'
    empCount = 0
    def __init__(self, name, salary):
        self.name = name
        self.salary = salary
        Employee.empCount += 1
    def displayCount(self):
        print "Total Employee %d" % Employee.empCount
    def displayEmployee(self):
        print "Name : ", self.name, ", Salary: ", self.salary
```

Chapter 7: Importing Modules

In the previous topic we covered classes, which allow you to declare multiple functions and then call to them as needed thorughout the code. These combinations of variables and functions that can be called to form a nice, neat package which can make them much easier to deal with.

> "The best programmers are not marginally better than merely good ones. They are an order-of-magnitude better, measured by whatever standard: conceptual creativity, speed, ingenuity of design, or problem-solving ability."
> - Randall E. Stross

What Are Modules?

Now, what are modules? They are generally definitions of variables, functions, and classes. Think of them as the next rung on the ladder. Multiple classes can be contained within functions, and multiple functions can be contained within modules. A module looks very similar to any other Python program that you might code, and often contain large portions of code that might be called to throughout a larger program.

Modules were created because when you quit the Python interpreter and then attempt to enter it again, your created functions and variables that were read by the interpreter will be lost. When writing a longer program this can be a very serious issue. The longer your program gets –the more you want to separate the blocks of code so that you know where to access those blocks and can use them several times throughout your program.

Modules are files that contain Python definitions and statements. They are typically appended with the suffix .py, which you may have to use when calling to the file. The name of the module (a string) is available as a global variable.

Defining Modules

Modules are different because they allow you to import all of the module, or bits of the module into other programs. Create a new file named moduletest.py, and then input the following code; Your average module might look like this;

```
# Define variables:
numberone = 1
ageofgrandma = 79
# define some functions
def printhello():
print "hello"
def timesfour(input):
```

```
print input * 4
# define a class
class baseballCard:
def __init__(self):
self.brand = raw_input("What brand is the card? ")
self.player = raw_input("What player is on the card? ")
self.price = raw_input("How much did it cost? ")
self.age = raw_input("How old is it (in years)? ")
def printdetails(self):
print "This card is of " + self.player + ",
print self.brand, "card, of " + self.player, "is " + self.age +
"years old and costs
" + self.price + " dollars."
```

Looks pretty familiar right? It looks like any old Python program that you might code. Now, you can import specific sections of code from any module, which can then be used within your programs. In order to import portions of code from a module, you must use an import operator. If you wanted to important an entire module, it is relatively simple;

```
### mainprogam.py
### IMPORTS ANOTHER MODULE
import testmodule
```

Keep in mind that in this example, we are assuming that the module is located in the same directory as the mainprogram.py file. But, you can also import very specific segments of your program as well. This is great for when you want to call on a specific class or variables that are contained within your modules.

Import statements are most commonly contained within the beginning of a Python file, but can technically be found anywhere within a program. Here is an example of calling on specific portions of code contained within a module;

```
### USING AN IMPORTED MODULE
print testmodule.age
baseballCard = moduletest.baseballCard()
baseballCard.printdetails()
```

This is a straightforward example of how you can call on various aspects of a module from your main program. You can import either your whole module, or very specific parts of the module. You can even call on global values of a module, and assign them to your program locally. An example of this would be;

```
# Assigning to a local name
timesfour = moduletest.timesfour
```

This assigns the value given by the "timefour"function and assigns it to a local variable. This is great for when you want to take global variables and give them a local assignment. This can make variables easier to call to, without having to call the module as a whole.

Python modules should be relatively simple for you to

understand at this point. Modules provide you with yet another organizational technique that give you more control over your program as a whole. You can use them to create increasingly complex programs, without feeling overwhelmed by the amount of code that you are creating. Splitting programs up into classes, functions and modules makes it easier to organize your code and gives you a consistent way to call to certain blocks of code that may need to be used throughout your program.

PROJECT: Modules

Use our previous example as a guide. Create a module that stores information about movies. One class, titled "movieInfo" should contain relevant information about the movie including the name, director, star, runtime (in minutes) and price. Have these values stored using raw_input. Also create a function that then prints those details.

Answer:

```
# define a class
class movieInfo:
def __init__(self):
self.name = raw_input("What is the name of the movie? ")
self.director = raw_input("What is the name of the director? ")
self.star = raw_input("Who stars in the movie?")
self.runtime = raw_input("What is the runtime of the movie?
```

```
")
        self.price = raw_input("How much did the movie cost?
")
def printdetails(self):
print  self.name + self.director + self.star + self.runtime +
self.price
```

Chapter 8: File I/O

Now that you know how to load external code into your programs, we will look into file input and output with normal text files. This is ideal for when you would like to store information in a text file, call for information from that text file, or use it in a variety of ways. File I/O commands are important, and used in any large scale Python program.

> "Talk is cheap. Show me the code."
> - Linus Torvalds

What is File I/O?

File I/O refers to using (inputing and outputing) data using normal text files. There are a number of commands and functions built directly into Python that allow you to create, open, append, and call to text files and the information stored on them. You can pass parameters, and use them as data dumps that can be called to at a later date.

Let's take a look at some of the basics of File I/O now, and look at how they might be used in the programs that you create.

Opening Files

In order to open files, you will be using the open() function. It is fairly self explanatory. You pass peremeters to the open() function, telling it how you would like it to open the file. A few of the different parameters that you might pass to the files include;

- **r** – for read-only files.
- **w** - for write-only files.
- **a** – for appending files.
- **r+** - for both reading and writing files.

These same parameters are present throughout your operating system and in other programming languages as well. Opening a normal text file is relatively simple and straightforward. Here is an example of opening a file using Python;

```
openfile = open('pathtofile', 'r')
openfile.read()
```

This instructs the program to open a file at a given path and then read the contents of that file. The text in .txt files is completely unformated. You can also print the information that the program reads with the following code;

```
print openfile.read()
```

This allows you to display any of the data that is stored within the text file. Try typing this into your IDE now.

Did it work? Probably not. We are introducing a new concept that has not yet been covered in this book. You failed to print the read data because the cursor had changed positions. "Cursor? What Cursor?"you are probably asking right now.

Cursor

A cursor is an unseen market of where the program will read functions from (along with other I/O functions), letting it know where to start from. In order to set the cursor where you need it to be, you must use the seek() function. The seek() function is used in the following form;

seek(offset, whence)

- **Whence -** Whence is an optional inclusion within the seek() function. When the whence is 0, the program will read and count all of the bytes and letters contained within the text file from the very beginning. When it is set to 1, the bytes will be counted from the current position of the cursor. If it is set to 2, then the bytes are counted from the end of the file only. When there is nothing in its stead, 0 is assumed by the program.
- **Offset** –The offset describes how far from whence the cursor movies. So for example, an offset of openfile.seek(45,0) would move the cursor 45 bytes from the beginning of the file. An offset of openfile.seek(10,1) would move the cursor 10 byes from the current position of the cursor. Negatives can also be used, which denote the position from the end of the file. For instance, openfile.seek(-77,0) would

move the cursor 77 bytes behind the end of the file.

This may seem overly complicated of reading.txt files, and it definitely is for the basic commands. But, this function provides deeper functionality, allowing you to determine where the program begins reading the file from. This provides versatility when working with.txt files.

Other I/O Functions

There are a large number of different I/O functions that you can call on and use when dealing with .txt files. These functions include;

tell()

Returns where the cursor is currently located within the file. There are no additional parameters with this function. It is useful for determining how your code is effecting the placement of the cursor, and provides added control. You can access it by typing fileobjectname.tell() - with fileobjectname being the name of the file that you are opening. The position of your cursor may change as your code runs, and tell() is very useful for examining how your code effects the placement of that cursor.

readline()

This function reads from where the cursor is currently located until the end of the line. The end of the line is not the edge of the screen, it is where "enter"is hit, creating a new line in a .txt file. Remember that an individual line can go on an unlimited amount in a text file. There are no parameters that need to be passed when using readline().

For instance, if you had an example text file that looked like this;

Line 1

Line 3

Line 4

Line 6

The returned list would look like this;

Index 0 = Line 1

Index 1 = "

Index 2 = Line 3

Index 3 = Line 4

Index 4 = "

Index 5 = Line 6

Each line in a .txt file constitutes a different index within the code. This makes the placement of your data predictable.

When you want to create a new line, you use the following command: "\n"at the end of any string.

write()

The write() command, as you might guess, is used to write data to the file. It writes from the position of the cursor, and will overwrite any text that comes after it. If you would like to add information to the end of the already stored data, make sure that your cursor is set to the end of the file.You can also use writelines() for writing multiple lines to a single .txt document.

close()

Close is typically used to close the file that it can no longer be used for reading or writing the data. The close() command is one that can help you to ensure that data is not inadvertently edited past the pont that you would like it to be.

PROJECT: File I/O

Using our previous examples, create a document, newfile.txt that says "Hello world" on one line, and "Hello FileI/O" on another line, then read it and print it.

Answer:

```
file = open("newfile.txt", "w")
file.write("hello world in the new file\n")
file.write("and another line\n")
file.close()
file2 = open('newfile.txt', 'r')
print file2.read()
```

Chapter 9: Error Handling

All programs have errors. It is of the utmost importance that you know how to handle errors, exceptions, and problems and give you a good idea of how to go about fixing those errors should they arise. Error handling is important for usability.

> "When someone says: 'I want a programming language in which I need only say what I wish done', give him a lollipop."
> - Alan J. Perlis

What Is Exception Handling?

Exception handling is the process of handling errors, exceptions and problems. There are a number of different errors that are commonly seen in nearly any program. By default, programs have certain error codes that they will provide to the programmer, depending on what the error is. Of course, you want to make sure that when errors do arise (for both the programmer and the user) that the error messages are descriptive and give some idea of what the issue might be.

Some of the different types of errors and exceptions that you might deal with on a day to day basis include;

Bugs and Human Errors

Bugs and human errors are the most common problems that you willr un into throughout your programming career. Exception handling begins with gaining a deeper understanding of the different types of codes that will be output by the program when it runs into an issue. Here is what an error message might look at.

Traceback (most recent call last):

File "/home/ryan/errortest.py", line 8, in -toplevel-

answer = menu(< I'll snip it here >)

File "/home/ryan/errortest.py", line 6, in menu

return raw_input(question) - 1

TypeError: unsupported operand type(s) for -: 'str' and 'int'

Now, this probably doesn't look too straightforward to programmers that do not have a lot of experience. Python is telling you a number of different things here. Look at this line;

File "/home/ryan/errortest.py", line 8, in -toplevel-

This line gives us some vital information. First of all, it lets us know which file the error occurred within. This is extremely important for larger programs that have a number of different modules. Without this, it would be difficult to determine exactly where the error might be.

It then tells us what line the error is located on. This lets us know the first place we should look for the issue. Keep in mind that the actual issue could come from another line within the code. Perhaps the line the error references is calling a variable that was never defined? There are multiple reasons why an exception could be triggered, and not all of them will be apparent just by looking at a single line of code.

```
TypeError: unsupported operand type(s) for -: 'str' and 'int'
```

This lets us know what type of error has been triggered by the system. This can provide clues as to what the issue within the code might be, which makes them quite easy to fix.

Exceptions

The other type of code error outside of human error is known as an exception. One example of an exception would be when you are asking for user input of a number. The code works fine when everything goes as expected. But what would happen if the user accidentally input a letter instead of a number?

Normally, this would cause the program to crash and all unsaved data to be lost. Instead of crashing, we want the program to recognize that the wrong type of data was entered, and re-prompt the user to enter the correct type of data.

Here is an example of how you would go about handling this exception using the ValueError command;

```
while True:
    try:
```

```
        x = int(raw_input("Please enter a number: "))
    break
except ValueError:
    print "Oops! That was no valid number. Try again..."
```

Exception handling can be successful when using the try statement. There are a number of reasons for this including;

- The try statement is executed.
- If there is no exception, the clause is then skipped and the programs executes as would normally be expected.
- If an exception occurs during the execution of the clause, then the clause is skipped. In this case, if the program generated a "ValueError"exception, the print command would then be executed and the program would prompt the user for input again.
- If an exception is generated and does not match the "ValueError"exception, it is then passed to outer try statements that might exist. If there are no outer try statements, this is known as an *unhandled exception*.

Conclusion

So, now you've learned the basics of Python. You've learned about and put into practice all of the basic concepts to get you going including data types, decision making statements and loops. Your in a good place to quickly grow your skills. From here on out, you have to challenge yourself! Python is a deep language with quite a bit to learn, but with a basic understanding of the fundamentals the more advanced concepts can come quite easily.

Moreso than any other aspect of programming education – experience is your best friend! You can only become a better programmer when you are willing to put in the work and gain experience in the language of your choice. Once your skills in a single language are sufficient, you will find that transferring that knowledge to another language is much easier. While there are differences between object oriented programming languages (and other languages), they are for the most part very similar, with transferable skills and concepts.

This guide walks you through all of the basic concepts for programming in Python, and is meant to be a guide that helps you to learn the basics and expand your skills.

Python is a rapidly growing language that is used by some of the largest corporations around the world. Python programmers are in high demand, a trend which will continue moving forward.

Bonus 1: Programming Toolkit

Contents

INTRODUCTION

Coding is like a game of chess, only grander, and with chances of undoing moves. Like chess, coding relies on a select set of moves (think statements and functions) and a problem that has to be resolved by playing those moves until the goal is reached.

For new programmers the task of understanding the problem, breaking it down, creating a strategic coding plan, and then playing the statements to process the goal can become daunting.

Given how fast paced the app development process are: with short deadlines, and reliant on agile development with continuous update of project description, coders that write clean codes are the first choice for contractors. Then again, clean and easily readable code is faster to debug.

This guide will hand over various tools, device, and tips that will help you write better and faster code.

As a result, you can spend less time on your code, deliver results faster, gain better reviews and feedback from the clients, and build a more robust portfolio.

Writing Code

Programming is more an art than a rigid science —the reason why so many large projects fail to get off the ground or work. But as with any modern practice, time and a sense of finding scientific rules, has brought to the coding world various tried and tested methods of organizing a code from the beginning. Though accomplished programmers create their own unique methodologies for writing code, new programmers are well advised to begin with some of the more streamlined methodologies.

Some of the prime problems that you can face during that time is deciphering the problem right and starting out in the right direction for your coding journey. Coding is a long journey and problems in anything ranging from missing a coding glitch or not starting out in the right manner can cause serious problems for everything there is to know there.

This section will highlight the various methodologies currently being employed by the programmers and will help you overcome any problems that head your way.

Tested Coding Methodologies

New programmers should be aware of the multiple programming methodologies being employed by programmers. This will save you the trouble of employing absurd methodologies or combining multiple methodologies. Here's a first aid box for *starting to code* the right way on your program.

Spaghetti Programming

This is not really a methodology, but result that new programmers achieve with ease —a tangled mess of an original program that goes through multiple modifications to make it work. The programmers start by identifying a problem and creating a simple program for resolving a part of the problem and then moving ahead with multiple modifications. The result is a program without a proper flow, but that somehow works.

Structured Programming

Keep programs organized by dividing your program into three distinct parts:

- **Sequences** - Group of commands that the machine could follow consecutively

- **Branches** — All command groups that have a condition built into them, causing the machine to follow one of several other group commands over others
- **Loops** — group of commands dedicated to repeating a task indefinitely or a defined number of times

Planning the program beforehand in terms of the sequences, branches, and loops is best suited for short programs.

Top Down Programming

At times programs get lengthier and it becomes difficult to gain a panoramic view of the whole program. When this happens, programmers tend to break the program into multiple blocks, each defined by the *function* it is supposed to perform. The idea is that writing smaller chunks of programs is easier. You start by identifying the main tasks that your program must perform and then create smaller programs for each task. Finally, you paste them together like building blocks and integrate them in the main. This makes it easier to find and modify sub programs and hence make a better program.

Event - Driven Programming

Programming where the flow is determined by occurrence of events i.e. inputs from the user (touch, mouse clicks, key presses, etc) or inputs received from other threads or programs. Normally the program has a main loop that is divided into two sections: an event detection block and an event handler block. This drastically speeds up the response time of the application being developed.

Object Oriented Programming

Currently popular, when writing a code using this methodology, programmers define not just the data type of a data structure, but also the types of its functions that can be applied to the data structure. As a result, the original data structure becomes a standalone object with data and functions. Later, the programmer can code relationships between two and more objects and build the program using these blocks.

The prime advantage of this programming method is that programmers can continue creating new objects without having to make any change to any module.

MAKING READING SIMPLER – BEST PRACTICES FOR WRITING READABLE CODES

Extensive Documentation

Explain your work. Add comments inside programming to show what direction you are taking: what a group of commands, or a chunk of code, is meant to do; why you've added it in the first place, and more. This makes it easier to read your code and see how each chunk of program connects with the other.

Standardize Indention and Naming Schemes

Indention makes it easier to skim through a program. It allows the reader to easily differentiate between conditions/loops and the code that is relevant to them or outside of them. Though it is not a requirement of most programming languages, it will allow you to better convey the structure of your programs.

Employing a standard naming scheme for declaring variables, classes, functions, etc, creates symmetry and makes it easier to spot a problem lines away. Two popular choices include using underscores between strings/characters (e.g. first_variable_name), and in case of not leaving spaces, capitalizing the first *letter* of every word except the first word (e.g. firstVariableName)

Group Codes

Use comments to separate blocks of code, no matter how small. More often than not, a task requires very few lines of code, and hence can become easily lost in the sea of code. To prevent this from happening, simply create separate blocks by adding a space followed by a short comment before the start of the block.

Do No Evil

Often known as the DIE (Duplication is Evil) and DRY (Don't Repeat Yourself), it is a principle that reminds programmers of the fundamental purpose of writing codes: to automate repetitive tasks. In a phrase, the same piece of code should never be repeated in your code.

Set a Line Limit

Make it easier to read your code. Avoid writing lengthy horizontal codes. Standardize the characters you want for a single line of code then break the line and start in the next. Writing codes in vertical, column like (newspaper like), form makes reading more comfortable for our eyes.

Select the Right Methodology

Nowadays, object oriented programming is a norm for creating well-structured programs. But at times, structured and procedural programming can prove beneficial. A good rule of thumb is to use objects when data representation is involved (e.g. data from a database), whereas, structured programming may be use for tasks that can be performed independently.

SOLOMON ON DEBUGGING –BEST PRACTICES FOR DEBUGGING CODES

The 9 Rules of Debugging

Dave Agans, near legend software developer and holder of various customary titles, once stumbled upon the Wisdom of Solomon (while Solomon was debugging programs). Here are the 9 rules that will get you through any debugging trouble you're likely to face.

- Understand the system
- Make it fail
- Quit thinking and look
- Divide and conquer
- Change one thing at a time
- Keep an audit trail
- Check the plug
- Get a fresh view
- If you didn't fix it, it isn't fixed

Let's see each in brief:

Rule	What You Need to Do
Understand the system	This holds true especially in case you are working with a code that's running on a specific platform or device. • Understand how the system processes the code by thoroughly reading the instruction manual. • Know the roadmap for the code. You must know what functions are where and how the coding blocks and interfaces do. • Know the tools you'll be using and how they debug.
Make It Fail	Learn all the instances where the program fails. This lets you focus on hypothesizing for probable causes. It's like knowing how you can make a sane program generate the same error again. But don't rely on this if the problem is intermittent i.e. it happens only once in a while. In case of intermittent failures, check for uninitialized data, multi-thread synchronization, timing variations, random data input, etc.

Quit thinking and look	The worst thing you can do is to rely on your intuition. Guesswork is a capital mistake. It makes you twist the debugging process to verify or falsify your guesswork. It's a waste of time, and most of the code you've changed will end up creating more trouble later. • See the error occur in person • Find the details. Don't guess which code block is the culprit, find the lines. • Guess only to focus the research.
Divide and conquer	It's hard for the bug to remain hidden if its hiding place keeps getting cut in half. Find the problem by narrowing the search with successive approximation i.e. find the range of possibilities where the bug could have occurred. Start on the worst hit parts and fix the bugs that clearly shout out their presence. Don't forget to fix the small noisy bugs that make the system go haywire.
Change one thing at a time	Make the process predictable. Remove any changes you made that *did not* return the expected result. Your task is to isolate the key factor, and understand it before pulling the guns on it.

Keep an Audit Trail	Make not of what did, in the exact order as you did, and what happened when you did it. Always correlate events, and no matter how horrible the moment, note it down.
Check the Plug	Avoid falling into the trap of obvious assumptions. They often prove to be wrong. Always question your assumptions by checking them for bugs in the first place.
Get a fresh view	Take a break. Don't shy away from asking for help or asking for insights from others. Bugs happen, and your task should be to take pride in *getting rid of them*, and not "getting rid of them yourself!"
If you didn't fix it, it ain't fixed	Test and retest, and verify if it's really fixed. Keep in mind that a bug *never* goes away on its own. If you think you've fixed it, take out the audit book and *make it fail* like it never went away *yourself*.

The 80/20 Rule

80% of the results come from 20% of effort and 80% of effects come from 20% of causes. Period.

The 80/20 rule states that 80% of the results come from 20% of the causes, and 20% of the results come from 80% of the causes. This rule is also known as the Pareto principle.

Various examples of this rule are floating around the marketplace. Here are the ones that relate to the development process:

- 80% of the code is running 20% of the runtime.
- 20% of the code is running 80% of the runtime.

This means that whatever code you have with you right now, and which needs debugging, has a small part that is running most of the time, but a bigger chunk of it that is nor running all the time.

Coding Lesson: You should not assume that debugging, or project's progress, is ever linear.

[EXAMPLE]

Become Disciplined

Approach debugging as a process, and not a series of random trial and error steps. You can't count on your luck by tweaking some knobs in the code and *hope* to stumble on the bug. Rather, make it a habit to *follow* the code's execution process. Is the first block getting the input that it needs to produce an output for block B? Yes?, move on. No? Start digging.

Debug Other People's Code

Coding is like communicating your opinionated solutions to a problem. It always has some assumptions, and which most likely causes errors to occur. If you find yourself stuck at debugging your own code, take a whiff of someone else's code (think cross-peer debugging and cross-peer code reviews). By debugging someone else's code, it becomes easier to figure out assumptions that other people have made. This in turn can bring to light some of the ones that you had left out during your debugging process. Furthermore, peer-review debugging sharpens your ability to pinpoint common causes of defects more quickly, and as a result teaches you to recognize (and abandon) your own bad development practices.

Think like a Compiler

This is something that must be done before you hit the compile button. This is an exercise in correcting as many errors before you let the IDE's integrated debugger to create the program. The fact of the matter is that you'll learn less from compiler's automation whereas by consciously examining the process will give you more depth to the basic debugging process, and hence common errors.

Debug the System and not Part of Blocks of Code

It's a mistake to start debugging by focusing only on part the code. Always pay attention to the interrelationships between modules, which is only possible if you have internalized the "9 rules of debugging"mentioned earlier. A rule of thumb is to read the code at multiple levels of abstraction i.e. spend time understanding what multiple pieces of the code are actually doing *together*.

CODE BLUNDERS:
AVOIDING THE FATAL MISTAKES

Over the years, programmers have come to acknowledge some common mistakes that brings home the message: it's not about how accomplished you are. Here are the top 8 mistakes that are made often and which can trouble your to no end:

Undeclared Variables

```
int main()
{
  cin>>b;
  cout<<b;
}
```

In the above code, the variable "b"has not been declared. There is no memory location for that variable, and hence, the compiler cannot send or fetch information from the location "b". This is rectified in the code below:

```
int main()
{
  int b;
  cin>>b;
  cout<<b;
}
```

Uninitialized Variables

Not all languages automatically initialize a declared variable to zero
e.g. C++

```
int variable;
while(variable<100)
{
  cout<<variable;
  variable++;
}
```

The above program will not enter the loop because the integer
variable has not been assigned a fixed initial value.

Hence the program would print all numbers within **int** range.
Always remember to initialize your variables.

```
int variable =0;
while(variable<100)
{
  cout<<variable;
  variable++;
}
```

Assigning a Variable to an Uninitialized Variable

Look at the code below where two integers are added

```
int y, z;
int add=y+z;
cout<<"Enter the two numbers you want to add: ";
cin>>y;
cin>>z;
cout<<"The answer is: "<<add;
```

The result of this program will be garbage values because the compiler does not know the basic equations like we do. Once you have assigned a value to a variable, that value remains till the end of times unless you reassign them. In the example program, because **y** and **z** are not initialized, **add** will always equal some unknown number no matter what number you decide to input.

Here's the fixed code:

```
int y, z;

int add; //initialized//
cout<<"Enter the two numbers you want to add: ";
cin>>y;
cin>>z;
sum=y+z;
cout<<"The answer is: "<<add;
```

Undeclared Functions

```
int main()
{
  something();
}
void something()
{
  //...
}
```

What is *something?* Unknown error.

You're assuming that the compiler will dig out information on what and who menu() is. It won't, not unless you declare it yourself. Always remember, either enter a prototype for a function, or define it in full *above* o *before* the first time you give a run for the memory.

```
void something();
int main()
{
  something();
}
void something()
{
  ...
}
```

Will know what something is like it's best bud.

Adding Extra Semicolons

```
int trying;

for(trying=0;trying<100;trying++);
  cout<<trying;
```

Output is 100. Always.

Semicolons have no place after loops, *if* statements, and/or definitions of *functions*.

```
int trying;

for(trying=0; trying<100; trying++)
  cout<<trying;
```

Overstepping Your Array Boundaries

There are limits that you must never cross:

```
int array[25];

//...

for(int boundaries=1; boundaries<=10; x++)

  cout<<array[boundaries];
```

Where are correct values? Lost in the digital void...

Arrays begin indexing at 0 and they always end their indexing at length-1. Period. Hence if you place a 25 element array, then the first position is at zero and the last one is at 24. So if you want to see your buddy "25":

```
int array[25];

//...
for(int boundaries=0; boundaries<10; boundaries++)
  cout<<array[boundaries];
```

Misusing the operators: || and &&

```
int value;
do
{
  //...
  record= 27;
}while(!(record==27) || !(record==43))
```

This code makes the program loop round like a record baby...

The only time that the while loop in the above can be wrong is when both record==27 and record==43 are true, and as a result cause the *negation* of each to be false i.e. making the || operation return false.

The code above offers a tautology: it is always true because the **record** can never hold both the values at the same time. Hence, if the program was suppose to *only* loop when the value entered for **record was neither** 27 nor 43, then it is necessary to use:

&& : !(record==27) && !(record==43).

This means "if **record** *is not equal* to 27 and **record** is *also not equal* to 43".

Programmers often mistake this logic by stating it as it is "this" or "that", while completely ignoring that the "other than" also applies to the entire statement and the two terms individually. This means you need to revisit the basics of Boolean algebra here!

No matter, the proper way to write the program is as follows:

```
int record;

do
{
 //...
  record=27;
}while(!(record==27) && !(record==43))
```

WHAT EVERY PROGRAMMER/CODER MUST HAVE

Tools for Boosting Productivity

WorkRave

Programming is "all-consuming"and it's easy to get caught up in the work. Though not a bad thing, working all day on a computer can start affecting your health and well-being. WorkRave forces you to take mini-breaks for your eyes and wrists. After a set time period, the program reminds you to give yourself a rest, grab a coffee, take a stroll, or any other non-computer related task.

Link: www.workrave.org

Blinklist

A real computer geek is rarely satisfied with only one computer. True that, but syncing multiple machines is a pain. Blinklist makes it easier to share bookmarks as well as note from anywhere.

Link: www.blinklist.com

CCleaner

Make your computer a lean mean development machine with this gig. Using your computer for extended periods can lead to accumulation of a lot of junk. It slows it down. CCleaner is the software that keeps your computer registry and other useless space hogging programs. Being on your computer all the time can lead to the accumulation of a lot of junk that can slow you down.

Link: www.piriform.com/ccleaner

EditPad Pro

It's hard to imagine a programmer who has not relied on the Notepad to do some of their work. After all, it's simple and gets the job done. EditPad Pro kicks the functionality several notches up. It grants you the ability to switch between files using tabs. It also offers a kind of "back in time"feature that lets you return to your previous editing position. Never lose your place with this tool!

Link: www.editpadpro.com/editpadlite.html

Filezilla

FTP is an incredibly useful tool for uploading websites and sharing files. Filezilla is your free FTTP tool offering standard features like drag and drop, resume, among support for a variety of transfer protocols.

Link: http://filezilla.sourceforge.net/

Inspector File Recovery

It happens to even the best of us: we're working happily on a project and forget to save a file, or horrifyingly "SHIFT +

DELETE"and later realize how important it was. Inspector File Recovery is the answer to all such day-mares and nightmares. This program can bring the files from the depths of the recycle bin *even when* your boot sector is damaged and headers are missing. Save your heart the shock and download it today!

Link: www.pcinspector.de/

KeePass

Forget your passwords? Perhaps because you have so many of them? KeePass makes brain cramps of such a thing of the past. It can keep track of all your passwords and make it easier to remember just one password.

Link: www.keepass.info/

MediaMax

No matter how many terabytes you have on your computer, you can't call it unlimited, or even risk free. Give yourself a storage boost of up to 25 GB with MediaMax, a free web-based app called MediaMax.

Link: www.mediamax.com

Plaxo

Keep your contact information updated and synched on all your smart devices with Plaxo. It automatically updates any contact information that you update in your email client by storing it (and updating it) on Plaxo's servers.

Link: www.plaxo.com

Ta-Da List

Staying orderly when the programs wont debug the right way can become challenging even for the most diligent of workers. Ta-Da List helps you out by keeping all your written tasks in order and accessible from any computer you use.

Link: www.tadalist.com

Tools for Better Project Management

Wunderlist

A wonderfully simple and basic task management and to-do list application. It allows you to create multiple to-do lists, create detailed tasks, add reminders, and more. It also allows you to sync your tablets, smartphones, laptops, and PCs. The paid pro tier allows addition of sub-tasks, emailing/printing, and sharing tasks to other workers.

Link: www.wunderlist.com

Remember the Milk

Another basic task management app that offers extensive online support through their website as well as iOS, Android, and Blackberry apps. You can easily integrate it with your existing Twitter, Gmail, and Outlook accounts as well as Evernote and Google Calendar.

The app will remind you through email, instant messages, and texts about your priorities and tasks. Furthermore, you can even share the tasks or decide to manage them offline as well.

Link: www.rememberthemilk.com

Toodledo

This is a full feature task management app with hotlist features for determining your high priority tasks, fine tuning of your tasks, and multiple filters, and a robust scheduler for planning your days (alarm included)

Link: www.toodledo.com

Producteev

This offers a big picture view of your tasks. It is a good solution if you need to manage tasks for multiple people but are not ready for a full-blown management software. Create teams and assign tasks and deadline; add notes, track progress, and various other options to gain a panoramic view of the entire process.

Link: www.producteev.com

Google Tasks

This service streamlines task management and is best suited if you are heavily reliant on Gmail or Google Calendar in your day to day workflow. Tasks adds a task list to your Gmail. It's easily accessible, and lets you convert emails into tasks as well as import new tasks into Google Calendar.

Link: www.gmail.com/mail/help/tasks/

WHAT EVERY PROGRAMMER MUST KNOW

The Programmer's Bill of Rights

Experts have long concluded that working conditions that are normally available for programmers, no matter how high their salary package is, cripple them. Hence, Jeff Atwood, coder and programmer incarnate brought the coding world a preposition for adopting a Bill of Rights for programmers. It includes things that programmers must not be denied:

- Every programmer shall have a fast PC

- Every programmer shall have two monitors

- Every programmer shall have their choice of mouse and keyboard

- Every programmer shall have a comfortable chair

- Every programmer shall have a fast internet connection

- Every programmer shall have quiet working conditions

Programming requires focused mental concentration. Programmers cannot work effectively in an interrupt-driven environment. Make sure your working environment protects your programmers' flow state, otherwise they'll waste most of their time bouncing back and forth between distractions.

BONUS 2: Your First $1000 Online

Thank You For Reading This Book.
Your First $1000 Bonus Report
www.YourFirst1000.GR8.com

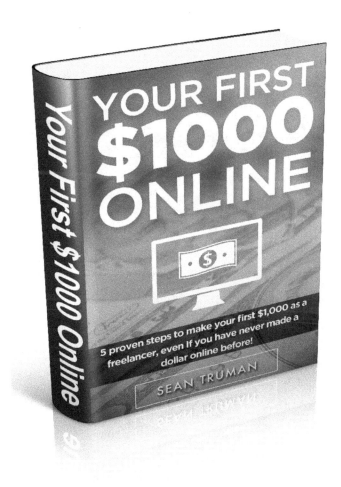

www.ingramcontent.com/pod-product-compliance
Lightning Source LLC
Chambersburg PA
CBHW061016050326
40689CB00012B/2660